IGNATIUS LOYOLA

by
Rev. J. A. Phillips SJ

All booklets are published thanks to the generous support of the members of the Catholic Truth Society

CATHOLIC TRUTH SOCIETY
PUBLISHERS TO THE HOLY SEE

Contents

The Standard of Christ 3

From Loyola to Montserrat 5

Years of preparation 11

Companions of Jesus 20

Workers in the vineyard 31

THE STANDARD OF CHRIST

2006 is a Jesuit Jubilee Year in which the 450th anniversary of the death of St Ignatius Loyola, the 500 years since the birth of St Francis Xavier and Blessed Pierre Favre, and the 400th year since the martyrdom, as a result of the Gunpower Plot, of St Nicholas Owen, Blessed Ralph Ashley, Blessed Edward Oldcorne and Fr Henry Garnet SJ are to be commemorated.

In this short biography of St Ignatius, Fr John Phillips SJ presents his life in vivid terms that demonstrate its heroism and variety. The son of a Spanish nobleman, St Ignatius was brought up at Loyola to the south of the Pyrenees, he spent his formative years in the household of the Royal Treasurer of Castile, and embarked on a military career with the Duke of Najera. He was injured in the Battle of Pamplona in 1521 and during his long convalescence at Loyola he experienced a conversion through reading the life of Christ and the lives of the saints. He surrendered his sword at the altar of Our Lady at Montserrat and went on to Manresa in 1552-3. There in solitude he made and wrote the *Spiritual Exercises* that led to the discernment of his future vocation.

After a period of education in Paris, in 1534 he and six companions made a vow of lifelong poverty and service to others. Six years later at La Storta outside Rome, after he had had a vision of himself being accepted as a servant, at the

Father's request, by Christ, who was bearing the Cross, he and the others put themselves at the disposal of the Pope. In 1540 the Society of Jesus was constituted by Pope Paul III.

Fr Phillips emphasises the military and chivalrous background to St Ignatius's life in a way that might seem strange to the modern mind. Yet both are integral to an understanding of him because by exchanging the pursuit of earthly arms for spiritual combat beneath the Standard of Christ against the powers of evil he formed an alliance that was essential to his vocation and ours. St Ignatius was a romantic in the service of the Kingdom of Christ, the eternal Lord of all. But he was also a realist eager to take up challenges in the service of the Church.

The same spirit of challenge informs the life of the Society of Jesus today. His spirit lives on in the Society but also in the lives of all who have made the *Spiritual Exercises*. The *Exercises* open a path to God. The Jesuits are contemplatives in action and the spirit of St Ignatius enables those influenced by the Society and Ignatian spirituality to become men and women for others. This involves generosity and courage in working to establish the Kingdom of Christ on earth, a kingdom of truth, justice and peace. These aims cannot be understood independently of understanding the life of St Ignatius Loyola, a soldier of Christ, and Fr Phillips presents it with freshness, vigour and conviction.

Anthony Symondson SJ

From Loyola to Montserrat

It is hard for people of the twenty-first century to form an accurate idea of the University of Paris as it was at the beginning of the modern era. We might be inclined to picture to ourselves some neat group of buildings standing in their own spacious grounds, something rather like one of our newer British Universities. Nothing could be further from the reality. Paris in the sixteenth century was divided into four well-defined areas. In the Seine stood La Cité - Paris proper, an island. On the northern bank, within the walls, lay La Ville, or the town of Paris. The southern wall enclosed the University. Outside the walls stretched the suburbs, in every direction. Such was the lie of the city. The University, therefore, was really a very important part of Paris, though almost an independent part; for only the University's own authorities, together with the Church, ruled there. The area covered by the University was small, but it contained no fewer than seventeen churches, fourteen monasteries, several hospitals, sixty colleges - some public, some private - and various lodgings, shops, and out-buildings. A probable estimate places the number of students in the early sixteenth century at twelve to sixteen thousand. These young men were gathered together from far and near - France, Spain, England, Italy, Germany, Turkey, Egypt, Assyria - from practically every part of the civilized world. They were there to study, of course, but many led a wild and riotous life, in which the very professors sometimes set the example.

Among the colleges was one called Montaigu. In the past it had not had a very good reputation. Erasmus had studied there, but it did not suit the finical scholar: the eggs were bad, the wine "mouldy," and there were other discomforts to spoil his delight in the ancient classics. But after his time it attained a high reputation for discipline and the good behaviour of its students. Attracted probably by this, a Spanish student came there in 1528 to continue his studies. He arrived in the very depth of winter, a short man, with a slight limp, in spite of which he had trudged through the snows all the way from Barcelona. He was poorly clothed, but bore himself with dignity. If you looked into his face, you found the features refined, though slightly haggard with fatigue. The forehead was high and rather broad, a forehead anyone might envy; the mouth and the chin were small, almost delicate, but strong, as you could see from the lips, which could close in a very determined line. But it was the eyes that held you: deep, dark, penetrating, yet kindly and understanding eyes, the eyes of a man who had suffered much and in his sufferings learned the great lesson of sympathy.

This man had been born in north-western Spain most probably in the year 1491. His father, Don Beltran, Lord of Loyola, had him baptized with the name of Inigo (in Basque, Eneco), in honour of St Eneco, O.S.B., Abbot of San Salvador at Ona, near Burgos. In later life Inigo adopted the name Ignacio, or Ignatius, apparently out of devotion to the martyr of Antioch. And finally Inigo de Loyola became St Ignatius Loyola, a name written indelibly across the pages of history for all time.

The raw material

About his youth and early manhood we have no details, but some indications of character and disposition have come down to us. They are enough to show that as courtier and soldier he was a man of his age, but a man capable of very disinterested service of a leader or a cause. He was fond of tales of chivalry and noble deeds. His admiration for a courageous and vigorous character was shown in his devotion to St Peter. This devotion to the Prince of the Apostles, however, did not mean that he was notably given to exercises of piety. He observed the ordinary obligations of Catholic practice, but he was a man full of ambition and vanity.

Yet, outwardly at least, he must have been an attractive figure, this young Spanish cavalier. From the age of sixteen or seventeen he assumed military dress and wore corselet and gorget, and went about armed. His heavy black locks, crowned by a gay cap, fell freely about his shoulders, forming a broad frame for the swarthy young face with its vivacious eyes and quick lips. No one would easily have dared to offend him: he was sensitive of his honour and ready to defend it. What fire and energy he could display was revealed at the siege of Pamplona in 1521. The magistrates surrendered the town to the invading French forces, but Ignatius persuaded the commandant of the citadel to defy the enemy. The French attacked in vain, until the brave young captain fell wounded in both legs. The garrison then yielded, but the French, in admiration at his courage, refused to accept the surrender of Ignatius's sword, and gave him every attention they could. When he was somewhat recovered they sent him to the Castle of Loyola. There it was discovered that "whether the bones had been badly set at first, or whether they had been jolted on the journey," they were now so displaced that they had to be broken and reset. This was a very painful operation, but only the white gleaming knuckles of tightly clenched fists betrayed the patient's agony....

There followed slow weeks of feverish sickness, and even the iron constitution of Ignatius seemed to have reached the limits of resistance: his life was despaired of. He received the Last Sacraments on the vigil of St Peter and commended himself to the Saint. On the feast-day his illness took a sudden turn for the better and he rallied. It was then found that a piece of bone was causing an ugly protrusion below the right knee and that this wounded leg was shorter than the other. The vain young cavalier insisted on another operation to remove the deformity, and that the leg should be stretched in an iron frame. This defiance of pain was daring indeed, and his strength returned so slowly that more than six months passed after this third operation before he was well enough to move about freely.

Time to think

During these weary months he whiled away the time reading and dreaming. He wanted romances, tales of knightly valour; but none were at hand. They gave him, instead, a long life of Christ, and a collection of the Lives of the Saints. Sheer tedium forced him to read these, but, at first, apparently, they meant little to him. Gradually, however, he grew very fond of them and read them repeatedly. Again and again the thought of Christ's heroism and the noble gallantry of His Saints came back to him, and he began to argue with his usual daring: If St Dominic did this and St Francis did that, why should not Inigo de Loyola do as much? When the weary day had dragged to a close, he often asked that his couch be placed by the window, and there he would lie for hours, gazing into the star-jewelled depths of heaven. The grandeur of the mighty universe overawed him and gave the ideas aroused by his reading a grip, as it were, upon his soul.

But only little by little did he abandon his longing for worldly fame, his vanity, his ambition, and when he did so, it was only to be more ambitious still; for he then set the whole current of his being towards heroic sanctity.

"That which seems like magic in you..."

At last, in February, 1522, he was fairly well, and determined to leave the castle and set out on a new Crusade as a soldier of Christ. His father - and probably his mother too - was dead; for his eldest brother, Don Martin Garcia, was now Lord of Loyola. Ignatius had not been able to conceal altogether the change in his outlook upon life, and his brother, suspecting he was going to flee to some monastery or other, sought to dissuade him. He conducted Ignatius from room to room of the ancestral Castle and pleaded the great expectations that Ignatius had aroused, his abilities, and "that which seems like magic in you - the influence you exercise over all minds." A soldier might be a saint; let Ignatius stay with his relatives: they would place no obstacle in the way of his private devotions.... Ignatius saw that this would mean the placid acceptance of mediocrity, and replied that he must report to his captain, the Duke of Najera.

He reported and drew his pay, but then went to the famous Monastery of Montserrat, where he made a very detailed general confession of his life. He had his sword and dagger hung up at Our Lady's altar; for he was to fight no more for the honour and glories of this world, but for the great Queen of Heaven and her Son, the eternal Lord of all things. In the spirit of mediaeval chivalry he spent the vigil of the Feast of the Annunciation watching before the altar of Our Lady, and in the early morning he heard Mass and received Holy Communion. He then crept into hiding in the obscure town of Manresa, where he tried to put into practice all he had read in the Lives of the Saints: he tried to take Heaven by storm.

YEARS OF PREPARATION

The powers of evil seem to have realized that here was a man who might prove dangerous indeed. Ignatius was tried in many ways: tempestuous doubt and fear and diffidence assailed him, scruples racked him, suicide offered an avenue of escape from agony of mind.... But from it all he gradually learned the ways of the spiritual life and how to deal with the tricks and wiles of the "enemy of our human nature." The training had been intense and vigorous, but Ignatius was a good learner, and with God's help he fashioned from his own experiences one of the most powerful instruments ever conceived for the reformation and sanctification of human souls: the *Spiritual Exercises*, which aim at enabling the exercitant, with the help of divine grace, to order his life in accordance with the Divine Will.

Spiritual Exercises

The *Exercises* are arranged in logical and methodical order, so that their effect is, as it were, cumulative, and the sinner, impressed by the enormity of sin, is led to repentance and reformation, while the righteous are encouraged to a more generous imitation of Christ. In his now famous parable of the Kingdom of Christ, St Ignatius appealed especially to all that is highest and noblest in man's sentiments of chivalry. First of all I "place before my eyes," he says, "a human king, chosen by God our Lord Himself, to whom all Christian. princes and all Christian men pay reverence and obedience. Consider then how this king addresses all his people, saying, 'My will is to conquer all the land of the infidels; so, whosoever wishes to come with me must be content with the food, drink, clothing, etc., that I have. In like manner he must labour as I do by day, and watch by night, etc., so that he may afterwards share with me in the victory according as he has shared in the toils.'" St Ignatius then asks us - he credits us with generous inclinations - to consider what good subjects ought to answer to so liberal a king, to such a man indeed; and, consequently, if anyone should not respond to the call of this king, how he would deserve to be blamed by everyone and regarded as a knight unworthy of the name. "We know, as St Ignatius knew, the power and attraction of a great and commanding personality, the enthusiasm a capable leader can inspire, what men will do in his cause…. But, continues St Ignatius, "if we give heed to such a call of the temporal king to his subjects, how much more is it a thing worthy of consideration to see Christ our Lord, the eternal King, and before Him the whole world, upon all of whom and each one in particular, He calls, saying: 'My will is to conquer the whole world and all My enemies, and thus to enter into the glory of My Father. Whosoever, therefore, desires to come with Me must labour with Me, in order that following Me in hardship, he may likewise follow Me in glory.'" From his own experience St Ignatius knew that there would be many men who would not be content with loyal service of their leader in good fortune and ill, but would wish to signalize themselves in that service. "Those," he says, "who wish to make a more generous response and to be outstanding in the thorough service of their eternal King and universal Lord, will not only offer themselves entirely to toil, but, by going against their love of creature-comforts, against their earthly love of friends and their love of the world, will make offerings of greater value and consequence, saying:

> 'O eternal Lord of all things, before Thy infinite Goodness and in the sight of Thy glorious Mother and of all the Saints of Thy heavenly court, with Thy favour and help I make my offering, protesting that I sincerely desire, and that it is my considered resolution, to imitate Thee, in so far as it be to Thy greater service and praise, in hearing all injuries and insults and the want of all things, in practice as well as in spirit, if Your Most Holy Majesty chooses to accept me for such a life and state.'

Here is the fullness of 'vocation.' Ignatius, the new soldier of Christ, was not concerned with what he was leaving behind: he looked forward to what he might achieve-in himself and in others. 'Vocation' for him, 'vocation' for any generous heart, is not so much a sacrifice, a loss, as a gain. It is not negative; it is positive. It is not the emptying of life - it is its fulfilling: a stretching forward to the fuller possession and the complete enjoyment of the supreme and only source of joy, the Living God.

Naturally, therefore, the parable of the Kingdom of Christ is at the heart of the Society of Jesus, of that Society whose members take as their ideal the victory of Christ over His enemies and the spread of His Kingdom to the ends of the earth. For this they live and work and die-from the shores of the Indian Ocean to the icebound coasts of the Bering Sea.

Years of preparation

With the *Spiritual Exercises* Ignatius wrought much good in Manresa, but at last he decided that he must go on pilgrimage to Jerusalem, as some of his saintly heroes had done.

He set out in February, 1523, and after various adventures he reached the Holy City, where the Redeemer, Ignatius's new Captain-General, had died. Deeming nothing impossible, he thought he could tarry there and convert the Mohammedans to Christ, but the authorities knew the difficulties and dangers, and bade him return.

Back in Europe he was faced with the problem of his future. He believed that God expected much of him, but what could he do - a soldier, only able to read and write? He must have learning, so he took his place in the benches of a school in Barcelona and studied the rudiments of grammar for two years. In 1526 he went to the University of Alcala, but his zeal for souls and especially the wonderful effects of the *Spiritual Exercises* got him into trouble with the Inquisition: men thought that no ordinary means could work the marvellous transformations of life that Ignatius obtained by the use of the Exercises. The Inquisitors finally found him not guilty, but they forbade him to preach or work for the good of his neighbour's soul till he had finished his studies. This was too much for the saint: he moved to Salamanca. More trouble. On then to Paris, where he was left in comparative peace.

New friends in Paris

After studying classics for nearly two years at the College de Montaigu, Ignatius entered the College of St Barbara, where he shared lodgings with a brilliant young Spanish Professor of Philosophy, named Francis Xavier, and a clever student from Savoy, Pierre le Fevre commonly called Peter Faber. The latter was appointed to tutor Ignatius in philosophy. Formality soon dropped away, and the elder man began to learn something about his young master. Peter had been born, he found, in Villaret, near Geneva, in April, 1506. His parents were peasants, good people and religious-minded, but rather poor. As a boy, Peter had been sent to mind the sheep on the mountainside, but as he seemed an intelligent lad and begged to be sent to school, he obtained an education that fitted him to go to Paris at the age of eighteen. But the gay, careless, Parisian world, immoral enough, troubled the lad's sensitive and innocent soul, and made him a prey to constant uneasiness of mind. Ignatius soon won his confidence and was able to lead him to peace and strength of soul. Faber made the *Spiritual Exercises*, and then Ignatius revealed to him his plan of going to convert the infidels in the Holy Land. Gripped with sudden enthusiasm, Faber clutched hold of Ignatius and exclaimed: "I will follow you through life and death."

This first conquest was indeed worth while; for Peter Faber was a gentle soul, fine, generous; and compassionate.

One of his friends said of him: "There was a rare and delightful gentleness and grace in his behaviour towards others, which I never found in anybody else. In some way or other he became their friend, gradually crept into their souls, and by his conduct and his slow pleasant words kindled in them all an ardent love of God." After a splendid apostolate in Italy, Spain, and Germany, Peter Faber died prematurely in 1544. His friends were overwhelmed with grief at the loss of one they esteemed a saint. Francis Xavier, out in the foreign missions, seems to have felt that Faber was with him still: fearing for his ship in a most violent storm on the Indian Ocean, he cried out to his old friend to assist him from Heaven.

"The stiffest clay I ever handled"

This Xavier, Faber's great friend, was the second disciple that Ignatius gained. He came of a very noble family that had fallen on evil days during the futile wars between France and Spain. In Paris he lived in "wretched destitution," as he called it. Yet, at first, he seems to have looked down on Loyola, who, noble though he was, begged his food. Xavier was ambitious: he hoped to acquire fame in Paris and thus win some lucrative position that would restore the fortunes of his family. He was brilliantly clever, but at the same time fond of sport, and he spent many hours in racing and playing on the islands in the Seine. Yet, somehow, this gay and ambitious life did not altogether satisfy him, and Ignatius was quick to notice and interpret the sudden melancholy that would cloud the young professor's brow - he saw that here was a soul that would do great things for a great ideal. Therefore he set about gaining to his cause this man who almost despised him. He urged students to go to Xavier's lectures, he always spoke highly of him, and when Xavier found his pockets empty Loyola offered him money, which was actually accepted. Little by little

Ignatius won his confidence, until at last he was able to challenge him with the words of Christ, "What doth it profit a man if he gain the whole world and suffer the loss of his own soul?" Xavier resisted, his friends fought for him - one of them, Miguel Navarro, actually tried to murder Ignatius! But at last Xavier yielded to the skilful handling of "the one person-the words occur in a letter to his brother - the one person in all the world to whom I profess and acknowledge myself most deeply indebted for the inestimable services he has rendered me." Thus was won to the army of Christ that man who stands out in history as the greatest missionary the modern world has seen: the Apostle of India and Japan.

In passing, we may remark what a revelation of Loyola's character we get from his power to win over two such men as the gentle, sensitive Savoyard and the haughty, ambitious Spanish nobleman: two dispositions so diverse, both yielding to "that which seems like magic in youth. influence you exercise over all minds."

The next disciples to join Ignatius were two young Spaniards, who had come to Paris, not so much out of love of learning, as from a sincere desire to meet a man who bore, the reputation of a saint. The first of these two was Diego Lainez, a Castilian, whose great-grandparents had been converts from Judaism. He was quite young, only twenty, but his companion, Alonso Salmeron, was no more than eighteen. In spite of his youth, however,

Alonso was a clever Greek and Hebrew scholar. Within a few days of meeting their fellow-countryman these two young Spaniards had become his devoted disciples.

The fifth disciple, Simon Rodriguez, a Portuguese, was not hard to gain, as he already dreamed of going to the Holy Land to convert the heathen.

The last conquest was a Spaniard from Bobadilla in Old Castile. This man, Nicolas Alfonso, was an original character, energetic and daring - his companions thought him rather wild and rather too much of a talker. Like so many other university students of the time he was frequently in need of money. He became acquainted with Ignatius, who seems to have had something of a reputation as an almsgiver, and received both monetary and spiritual help from him. Finally, Bobadilla - he is usually known by the name of his native town - surrendered to the fascination of Loyola's zeal.

COMPANIONS OF JESUS

These six disciples knew each other well, but their dealings with Ignatius they had kept from one another: he had guided each one individually and in private. But, at last, when all but Xavier had made the *Spiritual Exercises*, Ignatius one day proposed that each one should now give up his life wholly to the service of Christ, his Captain and his King, and, in order to discover the best means of saving his own soul and the souls of others, give himself to prayer in an especial way for some days. On a certain day each was to meet Ignatius and give his decision. "You will find," said Ignatius, "that there are others willing to work with you." On the appointed day the six followers were astonished to find themselves together with their master. They were overcome with joy on finding that the promised companions were the very ones they themselves would have chosen.

Ignatius then expressed his own views to the little company. He desired, he said, to go to the Holy Land and there give himself to the conversion of Islam, and in order to bind himself the closer to God he was willing to take vows of poverty and chastity together with a vow to serve God in Palestine. He looked round at the others for their opinions, but each one declared that his ideas were exactly the same as those Ignatius had set forth. But what did poverty mean? They agreed that their vow of poverty would bind them when priests to give all their ministrations without accepting any stipend. And suppose they could not get to Palestine on account of the war with the Turks? They would wait a year in Venice, and if no ship sailed for the Levant during that time, they would then go to Rome and offer their services to the Pope. For the present, however, they would remain in Paris to complete their studies.

The first vows

In order to honour Our Lady and at the same time invoke her blessing, the seven friends fixed the coming Feast of the Assumption of that year, 1534, as the day on which they would take their vows. In the early morning of August 15th they left the University, crossed the Seine, and passed through La Ville into the northern suburbs. There they sought out the chapel of St Denis, which was on the slope of Montmartre about a mile from the walls and overlooking the city. The street in which stood this chapel of the Apostle of France is now named after Marie Antoinette, and a Convent of the Helpers of the Holy Souls (*Dames Auxiliatrices du Purgatoire*) now stands on the site of the ancient chapel, which was destroyed in 1795 towards the close of the French Revolution. The Convent, however, contains a restoration of the chapel and crypt* of St Denis. At the end 'of the street

---

* The crypt was not known to exist in St Ignatius's time: it was accidentally discovered by workmen only in the year 1611. The vows, therefore, must have been taken in the chapel itself, and not, as some writers assert, in the crypt beneath the chapel.

one comes to the almost interminable steps leading up to the wonderful Basilica of the Sacred Heart. This great church was France's act of reparation for the crimes committed by the revolutionary Commune of 1870, when the Archbishop of Paris and many priests and religious, including five followers of St Ignatius, were murdered.

But in 1534 these things were hidden in the distant future; what attracted the little band to the chapel was probably its association with the great apostle and martyr, St Denis. This was fitting: so many of Loyola's sons were to shed their blood for the Faith in every country of the world.

Peter Faber, who had recently been ordained and was the only priest in the group, said the Mass. At the Communion all pronounced their vows. Simon Rodriguez ever after retained a vivid memory of this event, which he recorded with great care. These are his words:

"Before giving the Holy Eucharist to his companions, Peter Faber took the Host in his hands, and turned towards them. Then, with their hearts fixed on God, kneeling on the pavement of the chapel, all, without leaving their places, pronounced their vows in a clear voice, so as to be heard by all, then they communicated. On returning to the altar, the Father, in his turn, pronounced his vows in a clear and distinct voice so as to be heard by everybody...."

The battleground

After the ceremony the seven went round the hill to the Fountain of St Denis, on the western slope, and there spent the day encouraging each other to generous service of God. Then they went back to their books and studies with the fresh energy aroused in them by their high motives: they would become learned men in order to serve God better, to spread more rapidly the Kingdom of Christ, and to combat ignorance and all the waywardness that springs naturally from it. And surely, if ever in the history of the world learned and holy men were needed, they were needed then. Christendom was breaking asunder: Henry VIII had just forbidden the Pope's title to be mentioned in England; Calvin was beginning to call upon men to pray to an inexorable God; and Luther was pondering over his Rhenish wine, trying to solve the problem why it was that the gospel of liberty, according to Dr Martin Luther, had only led to vast licence. Heresy, error, and vice were spreading far and wide. The battlefield was immense, but soldiers of the true Gospel were to gather in their thousands to the standard of Loyola and take a strenuous part in rolling the vast, unholy flood in confusion back upon itself. For that they would be hated and persecuted; men would try to drive them off the face of the earth, and all but succeed. Their hope, however, was not in men-how could it be? Their hope was in the Failure of Calvary, and they were to conquer as He conquered:

"...having joy set before Him, He endured the cross, despising shame, and now sits at the right hand of the Father."

The vows taken at Montmartre did not constitute the Society of Jesus; but the day of those vows has always been regarded as the birthday of the Society.

Jerusalem or Rome?

In April, 1535, Ignatius, having taken his Master's degree in Arts and having studied theology for about two years, was compelled by bad health to break off his course at the University and seek his native air. Once or twice he tried to resume his studies later on, but did not add much to what he had learned at Paris. His studies, therefore, had lasted eleven years. He had not studied for the sake of knowledge, nor did he find pleasure in his books. Those eleven years of study had been sheer hard work, and the only motive, the sole incentive through them all, had been the conviction that God's glory required him thus to fit himself for an apostolate. History tells of many men whose sheer strength of will amazes and awes us, but few, if any, can have surpassed, in self-sacrificing devotion to a cause, the application and perseverance of this man who gave himself so persistently to study in the face of poverty, persecution, and ill-health. He once remarked that he doubted if anyone else in the history of the world had ever made such sacrifices for the acquisition of knowledge as he had made. This was not boasting: it was a grim reminiscence.

The nine companions

While Ignatius was in Spain the six disciples continued their studies at the University of Paris, and met each year in the same chapel to renew their vows. The little band continued to grow, too; for it was joined by Claude le Jay from Savoy, Paschase Broët, a Frenchman, and Jean Codure, a Provençal from the Lower Alps. In 1537 the nine companions made their way to Venice, where Ignatius, restored in health, awaited them.

The pomp and splendour of the Republic of the Adriatic, Europe's most gorgeous mart, made no impression on Ignatius - he was not concerned with the ephemeral things of commercial life. Rather, he took the opportunity in Venice while waiting for his disciples to arrive from Paris to give the *Spiritual Exercises* to a young man named Diego Hoces. Diego was at first rather suspicious of these new-fangled things and began his retreat with a small library of the works of the Fathers, the decrees of the Councils, and so forth, at hand. His apprehension disappeared in a day or two and he enthusiastically joined Ignatius. Many others, even Venetian nobles, subsequently made the *Exercises*. These retreats not infrequently resulted in a vocation to the priesthood or the religious life, almost invariably in a complete change of life.

By special permission from the Holy Father, Paul III, Ignatius and the others who were not priests were ordained in Venice on 24th June, 1537.

Whilst waiting for a ship to take them to Jerusalem they worked in the hospitals or preached or taught in the streets. Their long wait was not rewarded: no ship would leave for the hostile East. 'Being free, therefore, from their vow of pilgrimage, they held a meeting and decided that Ignatius, Faber, and Lainez should go to Rome; the others would scatter through the University towns and preach to the students. Before they parted someone asked: "What shall we say to those who ask us who and what we are?" Ignatius replied: "Answer that you belong to the Company of Jesus: that will be our name."

"I will be gracious to you at Rome"

The Holy Father received Ignatius and his two companions with great kindness and gave them work to do.

The disciples labouring in the University towns and cities also found plenty to do. They lost at this time the last disciple to join, the little band, Hoces. He and Codure had gone to Padua where they worked with some success. One day Hoces preached in the great Piazza on the text, "Watch and pray; for you know not the day nor the hour." Almost immediately after the sermon he was attacked by a fever and, realized that his own day and hour were very near. He prepared himself for death, and soon passed to a better world. In life his swarthy face had been rather unpleasant to look upon, but Codure saw a strange fascination in the dead young face, which seemed to assume an otherworldly beauty. This so affected him that he wept for joy.

New Order

The companions, therefore, once more numbered only ten. As yet the nine disciples had no idea of forming a Religious Order. Polanco, who later became Ignatius's secretary, stated very definitely in his *Life* of the Saint, that "in 1538 they were still without any intention of forming any perpetual association or Order." But a number of young priests wanted to imitate their way of life, so Ignatius called all his followers to Rome. "We gave ourselves to prayer," Lainez wrote to a friend, "and afterwards we met together and weighed the circumstances of our vocation point by point. Each one set forth, as it seemed good to him, the *pro* and *contra* of the matter. In the first place, we were of one accord that we should found a society having a permanent existence and not one limited to the term of our natural lives." Thus, without directly suggesting it, Ignatius had allowed his disciples to reach the desire of a permanent society, and he was assigned the task of drafting a constitution for the new Order. When the outline was read to Paul III, he exclaimed: "The finger of God is here! We give this our benediction; We approve it and call it good." On 27th September, 1540, he issued a Bull - *Regimini Militantis Ecclesiœ* - formally approving and confirming the Society of Jesus. The pious association formed at Montmartre thus received the sanction of the Vicar of Christ and became one of the Orders of the Church.

The new Order contained several unusual features: the members were not obliged to wear a special habit or to recite the Divine Office in choir, they were to avoid ecclesiastical dignities and honours, and they were to take, besides the ordinary vows of poverty, chastity, and obedience, a fourth solemn vow pledging them in a special way to perform whatever work the Sovereign Pontiff might enjoin upon them. The ideals of the wounded soldier, dreaming in Loyola or praying in Manresa, had not changed: he had merely communicated those ideals and thus gathered round him a squadron of highly trained soldiers animated by his deathless ideals of heavenly chivalry, a squadron prepared to fling itself at a word from Christ's Vicar on any stronghold of the enemy, ready and willing to sacrifice all personal gain and comfort in order to establish the reign of Christ, our Lord.

The first Father General

As the Society was now a duly constituted Religious Order, a General had to be elected to govern and direct it. The election took place in Rome in the Lent of 1541. Xavier and Rodriguez, who had meantime been sent to Lisbon, left sealed votes in Rome. Faber sent his vote from Germany, but Bobadilla, who was. at Bisignano, did not learn of the election in time to forward a vote. The six companions actually in Rome also recorded their votes in writing. All voted for Ignatius Loyola, their leader, friend, and master. Some added a few comments to the ballot. Jean Codure, for example, wrote thus:

> With no thought but for the greater glory of God and the greater good of the whole Society, I vote for the man who in my judgment ought to be head and minister of the Society. That man and I bear witness that I have always known him zealous for the honour of God and most ardent for the salvation of souls; and he ought to be set over others for the reason that he has ministered to them and made himself the least among them is our honoured Father, Don Ignatius Loyola. And after him I choose a man not less endowed with virtue, our honoured Father Peter Faber. This is the truth before God the Father and Our Lord Jesus Christ; nor should I say otherwise even if I knew for certain that this, was the last hour of my life.
> *Jean Codure*

St Ignatius did not name anyone in his vote:

> Excluding myself, I give my vote, in Our Lord, that he may be our Superior who will be named by the majority of votes....If, however, the Society should think differently, and consider it better and more advantageous for the glory of God our Lord that I should name someone, I am ready to do it.
> Rome, 5th April, 1541.
> *Inigo*

But there was no need for his vote: not one of the disciples had the slightest doubt about the right man for the position. Ignatius himself, however, made some difficulty about accepting the office of General, and asked his followers to reconsider the matter carefully. A second election was then held, and again the vote was unanimously in favour of Ignatius. As the saint still showed himself reluctant, Lainez remarked, rather vigorously, "Father, yield to the will of God; for if you do not, the Society may dissolve itself, so far as I am concerned; for I am resolved to recognize no other than the head whom God has chosen." Finally, having consulted his confessor, St Ignatius yielded. The six companions in Rome then made their profession on Friday, 22nd April, of that year (1541), in the Church of St Paul-beyond-the-Walls. "St Ignatius said Mass in the chapel of Our Lady. At the Communion, St Ignatius, holding in one hand the Sacred Host, took in the other the formula of profession, and turning to his companions read it aloud. Then he communicated. He then turned to his companions, with five consecrated particles on the paten. They made their profession, and received Holy Communion at the hands of St Ignatius. Having made their thanksgiving after Mass, and prayed awhile at the privileged altars, they met at the high altar, and all embraced St Ignatius with the most tender affection." (Father Astrain, SJ)

WORKERS IN THE VINEYARD

During the years that he had known these men who formed the nucleus of the Society of Jesus, St Ignatius Loyola had gradually fashioned them according to his own generous and ardent spirit. He formed men whom he could send to the ends of the earth with the confident assurance that there the spirit he had imparted to them would issue in zealous service of God and man - in self-sacrificing toil for the salvation of immortal souls.

Fire upon the earth

And thus it was. The companions scattered far and wide over Europe and the world, and everywhere they went new fire burst forth and the Faith flourished.

Greatest and most wonderful toiler of all was Francis Xavier. After perils and sufferings without number he finally reached India in 1542. He took half Asia for his mission-field, and with incomprehensible energy laboured for the conversion of the heathen from the Fishery Coast to Malacca, and from Cochin to Japan. In all the history of the Church's growth no other missionary, except St Paul, leaves such an impression of superhuman energy and tireless devotion. For ten years he sought for souls in a thousand towns and villages of southern, south eastern, and eastern Asia. It has been estimated that his efforts gathered one million three hundred thousand souls into the fold of the Church.

And in the midst of these mighty labours Xavier's great heart burned with love for his distant friends, especially for his father in Christ, Ignatius, who under God had made him the apostle that he was. For example, he wrote from Cochin in 1544:

> I beg of you for the love of Our Lord God, dearest Brothers, to write to me at length about all the members of the Society; for since I no longer hope to see you face to face in this life, at least let it be as through a glass darkly, that is, by letters. And to Ignatius: So I close, beseeching Christ, since of His infinite mercy He has joined us together in this life, that after death He will bring us to His glory.

Again, eight years later:

> My True Father - I received a letter from your Holy charity at Malacca, when I got back from Japan. The news which I hoped for, and which it has given me, of the life and good health of one so dear and so venerated, has filled my soul with a joy known to God alone. I have read there many words breathing all your sweetness and piety; I have reread them many times for the comfort and the good of my soul. I go over them again in my mind, feeding on

them, so to speak, continually; especially those last words which are, as it were, the seal of charity, and which conclude your letter, "All thine, without the possibility of ever forgetting, Ignatius." I have read these words with tears of delight, and as I write them I weep at the blessed remembrance of past days, and of the sincere and holy love with which you have always enfolded me, and which still follows me...Your Holy Charity adds that you greatly desire to see me once more before the close of this life. Our Lord, who reads the depths of the soul, knows the keen and sweet emotion of tender love which this affectionate expression of your precious love has roused in my inmost heart. And as often as I turn over these words in my mind (which is very often) unbidden tears fill my eyes, and break forth gently and irresistibly at this one sweetest image on which my heart dwells, that it is possible I may again clasp you in my arms....

Having made mention of his vast debt of gratitude to Ignatius, Xavier turns immediately to that for which they both worked, the spread of the Kingdom of their eternal Lord:

In the name of the passionate zeal for the service and glory of Our Lord God with which you are animated, I ask one favour of you, which if I were in your presence I would implore before

> your holy feet on my knees: it is that you would send here some man thoroughly well known and approved by Your Holy Charity to be made Rector of the College of Goa. Such a man chosen by yourself, and so to say formed by your hands, is very much required by that College....

As he could not carry with him, in his mission journeys, all the letters of his friends, he cut off their signatures and kept these with him:

> In order that I may never forget you, I want to tell you, dearest Brothers, that for my consolation, as an ever-present means of recollection, I have cut out from the letters you have written me your names written by your own hands, and putting them together with my own vow of profession, I carry them about with me all the time for the sake of the great consolation that they give me.

Thus, in and through his wonderful friendship for Ignatius and his love for the Society of Jesus, Xavier was strengthened and encouraged to work wonders for the Church in India and Japan.

Come and help us

Moreover, seeing his vast mission-field white indeed unto the harvest, Xavier groaned in spirit and longed for more and more labourers to gather in the multitude of souls ready to accept the Faith.

> Often and often am I moved - he wrote in 1544 - to go to the Universities of Europe, and cry aloud, like a man who has lost his wits, most of all to the University of Paris, and say in the Sorbonne to those that have more learning than good-will to set about putting it to use: "How many souls will ye lose from glory and let go to Hell because of your neglect?" If they paid as much heed to the reckoning that God will exact of them, and to the talents that He has given them, as they do to their studies, many would bestir themselves, and take measures and the *Spiritual Exercises* so that they should feel God's will within their souls, and obey it rather than their own inclinations, and say: "Lord, here I am; what would'st Thou have me to do? Send me whither Thou wilt, even to India, if that be the thing to do." Thousands upon thousands of heathen would become Christian, if there were labourers minded to go to them... The multitude of people in this land who are ready to become Christians is so great, that it often happens that my arms are wearied out with baptizing, and that I cannot continue to repeat in their language the creed and commandments and prayers, and the explanation of what Christianity

means, and what Paradise is, and what Hell is, and who go to the one and who to the other....

There is nothing more to write to you concerning matters here, except that the consolation that God confers upon those who go among the heathen, converting them to Christianity, is such, that if there is content in this life, it is here....

Here, indeed, was a man who endeavoured to become the ideal knight to whom Ignatius appealed in the meditation on The Kingdom of Christ - a man who would give himself utterly to labour in toiling for the establishment of the reign of Christ our Lord upon the earth. A thousand such men would convert the world!

Abyssinia, the Congo and Brazil

The zealous work done by Xavier in Lisbon before left for the Indies so impressed King John III of Portugal that he asked that the Jesuits should be given a mission to Abyssinia, with which the Portuguese had friendly trade relations. The Pope approved, and St Ignatius agreed to do his best. But it was only after long delays that a band of twelve Jesuits - three of whom had been consecrated bishops - set out from Portugal in 1555. Through the scoundrelly fraud of a Portuguese adventurer, who had tried to persuade the Abyssinians that Paul III had appointed him Patriarch of Abyssinia, the missionaries found the country closed against them. Nevertheless, one bishop and five priests succeeded in penetrating into Abyssinia, where they laboured in the face of appalling difficulties and suffered with a heroism that must have been backed by an unusually great spirit of self-sacrifice and a marvellous devotion to duty.

In 1547 Ignatius had sent out a small expedition to the Congo, but the mission was not able to maintain itself on account of the rigours of the climate and the prevalence of tropical diseases.

An expedition to Brazil in 1549 was more successful and fresh parties of Jesuits were sent out, until, in 1553, St Ignatius was able to erect the Province of Brazil.

Thus, within the life-time of its founder, the Society of Jesus had penetrated India, the East Indies, Japan, Abyssinia, the Congo, and Brazil. That missionary spirit lives on and animates today the Jesuits who are labouring, with the dauntless chivalry of Loyola, in so many missions throughout the world.

In distracted Europe

In Europe itself the members of the new Order flung themselves into the work of the Catholic Church and the Counter Reformation with whole-hearted zeal and energy. In 1542 Salmeron and Broët were sent as Papal Legates to Ireland. They made their way into the country through Scotland, but, as there was a price upon their heads, and it was impossible to attain the objects of their mission, they returned to Scotland after spending thirty-four days in Ireland.

Peter Faber did great work in Louvain and Germany, Le Jay laboured in Bavaria and ether parts of Germany, and Bobadilla preached, taught, and wrote, in many famous German cities and also in the Austrian capital, Vienna, where part of his work was to prepare Jews and Turks for baptism.

When the Council of Trent opened in 1545, Lainez and Salmeron were sent as theologians of the Holy See, and Le Jay, to whom St Peter Canisius was later appointed assistant theologian, was present as procurator of the Bishop of Augsburg. At first, the Spanish prelates were rather ashamed of their fellow countrymen, Salmeron and Lainez; for they seemed very young for their position and their clothes were so shabby! But very soon the Jesuits had the enthusiastic favour of the Fathers of the Council, and Lainez was allowed to speak at great length. "Other theologians," Peter Canisius wrote, "have barely an hour to speak in; but Lainez was allowed by the Cardinal-President to speak for three hours and even longer." The splendid impression made by the four Jesuits at the Council helped to make the Society known, and many bishops asked to have some Jesuits sent to their dioceses.

Within a few years, therefore, the followers of Loyola had spread over Europe and the world. In the Eternal City stood Ignatius, directing, counselling, commanding, -

marshalling his ever-growing army to the service of its great Captain-General, Jesus Christ.

Ignatius himself toiled unremittingly, with incredible constancy and energy. Nothing that might redound to the greater glory of God was too much to ask of him. He undertook or directed the most varied good works in many parts of Europe, while, at the same time, his genius assisted from afar the distant missionaries of the Order. In spite of the vast burden he bore, Ignatius always showed himself serene and calm. His young friend, Ribadeneira, wrote of him, "If you wished to ask for something from Father Ignatius, it made no difference whether he was on his way from Mass or had had dinner, or whether he had just got out of bed, or had been at prayer, whether he had received good news or bad, whether things were quiet, or the world all upside down. With him there was no such thing as feeling his pulse, no taking a reckoning by the North Star, no steering by a sea-chart, as is the usual way in dealing with men in authority; for he was always in a state of calm self-mastery." And Gonzalez added that he was so completely inclined to love "that his whole behaviour seems love. And he is so universally beloved by all, that there is not a man in the Society who does not feel deep affection for him, and does not believe that Father Ignatius is very fond of him."

The spirit of the leader

His followers loved and reverenced Ignatius, and so they readily made his spirit their own. In 1547 he wrote an inspiring letter to the young students of the Order at Coimbra, a letter in which he sets forth at some length his ideals of the chivalrous service of God:-

> There is one thing I wish you to excel in above all others, and that is, that you be conspicuous in zeal for the glory of God, and the salvation of your neighbour whom Jesus Christ our Redeemer has bought at so great a cost. And, in very truth, are we not the soldiers of His company, in His special pay and under His special title? Special, I say; for there are many, general motives that induce us to further His dearest interests. All that we have, all that we are able to do, all is His gift. He it is who gave us being, He who furnishes us with all external goods. He who preserves us, our life, and the manifold perfections of our soul and body with all its parts. His, too, are the gifts of grace with which He has prepared us so liberally and lovingly, and which still flow out unto us, even after we have taken sides against Him. Out of His pure bounty, He has prepared for us and promised us riches beyond all valuing. He wills us to become joint possessors with Him in the treasures of His happiness, and to make

us, as far as possible, by the grace of adoption, what He is by His very nature. Lastly, the whole world is His gift, and all the fulness thereof, whether in the material or spiritual order. Not only has He placed everything under heaven at our service, but His own glorious court is to be ours....And as if all this were not enough, He has given us His own self as our reward, becoming our brother in the flesh, the price of our salvation on the cross, the support and companion of our pilgrimage, in the most Holy Eucharist. Oh, how mean-spirited that soldier must be, who is not moved to do stout battle for the honour of a King so generous! Certain it is, that to bring us to desire and promote this honour with a greater degree of affection and readiness, His Majesty has been pleased to prepare us with so many priceless and wondrous blessings. He has stripped Himself, in a manner, of His own consummate happiness and possessions, to make us partakers thereof. He has clothed Himself in misery, that we might be made free; He has willed to be sold, that we might be bought; dishonoured, that we might be glorified; made poor, to make us rich; and He died a death of ignominious torture, that we might live a life of blissful immortality! Oh, how ungrateful we are! What hearts of stone that, after all that has been done for them, are not, aroused to deeds of loyalty and heroism for the honour and glory of their Saviour Jesus Christ! Ignatius had lived his own ideals, and his great austerities and labours gradually wore down even his strong constitution. In 1550 he had a very serious breakdown in health, but recovered. In 1556, however, he fell ill again and knew that he must die - that his work was done. Polanco, his secretary, left a careful account of his last days on earth: told me it would be well if I went to St Peter's and had word sent to His Holiness that he was very ill and with no hope - or practically no hope - of life; and that he therefore humbly besought His Holiness to give his blessing to himself and to Master Lainez, who also was in danger of death; and that, if God our Lord gave them the grace of calling them to heaven, they would pray for His Holiness, as they were accustomed to do every day on earth. I replied: "Father, the doctors believe there is no danger in this sickness..." He said: "I am in such a state that nothing remains but to draw my last breath." Polanco then asked whether he might put off the visit to St Peter's till Friday - he had to catch the post to Spain. Ignatius replied: "I should prefer you to do it today rather than tomorrow, and the sooner you do it the better I should be pleased; but have it as you will, I place myself entirely in your hands."

Polanco consulted the chief doctor, who thought it there was no immediate danger. In the evening Ignatius "took a fair meal, considering what he was accustomed to take, and then conversed with us so calmly that I went with a quiet mind to bed, not suspecting any danger in his illness.

"The next morning at sunrise I found him *in exiremis* so I flew to St Peter's, and the Pope, who was overcome with grief, gave his blessing and all that his apostolic power could bestow, with sentiments of the greatest affection. And so, less than two hours after sunrise, in the presence of Dr. Madrid and Master Andres de Frusio, he placidly rendered up his soul to his Creator and Lord..."

Ignatius, the founder of the Society of Jesus, was dead. But his spirit lived on. It is living still, guiding and inspiring the lives of twenty thousand followers in every part of the world. Across the centuries, Ignatius Loyola still points the way to the ideal of spiritual chivalry. Faced with this ideal there will never be wanting generous hearts to respond by saying with Peter Faber, "I will follow you through life and death." Yes, through life and death, and beyond, to that deathless Life, where all noble hearts and all great deeds have their reward, the due reward of loyal self-sacrifice for the noblest and highest of all ideals the establishment of the Kingdom of Christ, the eternal Lord of all things.

Informative Catholic Reading

We hope that you have enjoyed reading this booklet.

If you would like to find out more about CTS booklets we'll send you our free information pack and catalogue.

Please send us your details:

Name ....

Address ....

....

....

Postcode ....

Telephone ....

Email ....

Send to: CTS, 40-46 Harleyford Road,
           Vauxhall, London
           SE11 5AY

Tel: 020 7640 0042
Fax: 020 7640 0046
Email: info@cts-online.org.uk